Volcanoes of the World ™

Mount Pelée
The Deadliest Volcano Eruption of the Twentieth Century

Kathy Furgang

The Rosen Publishing Group's
PowerKids Press ™
New York

For Adam

Published in 2001 by The Rosen Publishing Group, Inc.
29 East 21st Street, New York, NY 10010

First Edition

Series and Book Design: Michael Caroleo

Photo Credits: p. 1 © Phillip Gould/CORBIS; pp. 4, 12 © Archive Photos; p. 7 (illustration) by Michael Caroleo; pp. 8, 11 © National Geographic; pp. 15, 18 © CORBIS; p. 16 © North Wind Picture Archive; p. 20 © Paul Almasy/CORBIS.

Furgang, Kathy.
    Mt. Pelée : the deadliest volcano eruption of the 20th century / by Kathy Furgang.—1st ed.
        p. cm.— (Volcanoes of the world)
    Includes index.
    ISBN 0-8239-5663-6 (alk. paper)
    1. Pelée, Mount (Martinique)—Juvenile literature. 2. Volcanoes—Martinique—Juvenile literature. [1. Pelée, Mount (Martinique) 2. Volcanoes.] I. Title.

QE523.P3 F87 2000
551.21'09798'2—dc21   00-028591

Manufactured in the United States of America

Contents

Farmers in Martinique grow fruits, sugarcane, tobacco, and vanilla. In 1902, Saint Pierre was the largest city on Martinique.

Little Island in a Big Sea

In 1502, the famous explorer Christopher Columbus traveled to the Caribbean island that we now call Martinique. Warm weather and beautiful beaches make Martinique a wonderful place. About 100 years after Christopher Columbus visited the island, French settlers made it their home. What the French did not know at the time was that the island of Martinique is made mostly of volcanoes. Mount Pelée is a volcano in Martinique. The first people who discovered the volcano named it Mount Pelée, after the Hawaiian goddess of fire, Pele. In 1902, Mount Pelée became famous all around the world!

Mountain of Fire

There are three layers of Earth. The top layer is where we live. It is called the **crust**. The crust is made of solid rock. Underneath the crust is the **mantle**. This layer is made of solid rock and a very hot liquid rock called **magma**. Below the mantle, in the center of Earth, is the **core**. The core is the hottest place on Earth. The outside of the core is made of liquid iron and other **elements**. The inside of the core is a ball made of solid iron. When magma moves from the mantle into the crust, it is called **lava**. A volcano is a hill or mountain that is formed when lava breaks through the crust. When this happens it is called an **eruption**.

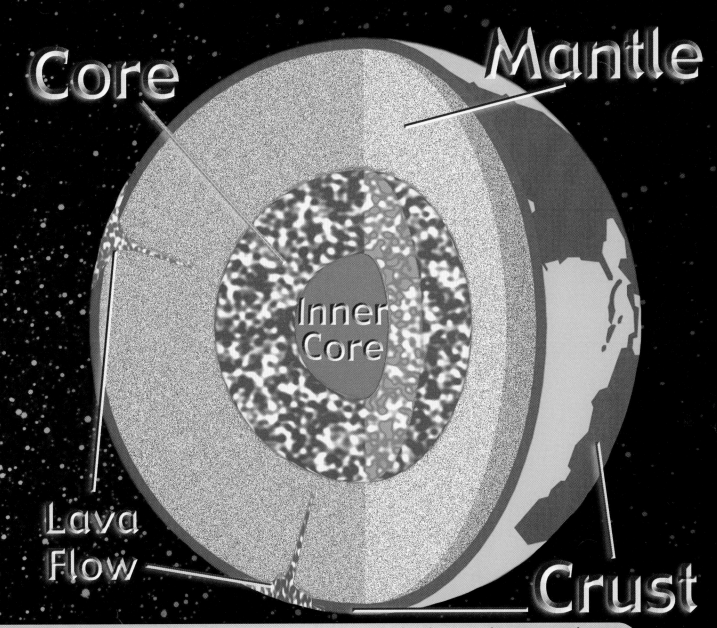

Core

Mantle

Inner Core

Lava Flow

Crust

Earth's crust is from 5 to 25 miles (from 8 to 40 km) thick. The mantle is around 1,800 miles (2,900 km) deep, and the core is around 2,150 miles (3,460 km) wide.

This picture shows a volcano that has risen out of the sea. More lava is layered on top of the volcano every time it erupts. This makes the volcano bigger.

Moving Plates

   Earth's crust is made up of parts called **plates**. These plates are always moving. They move so slowly that we cannot feel the motion. Sometimes when two plates bump into each other, one of the plates sinks down into the mantle. The part of the plate that is in the mantle melts and becomes magma. Imagine this happening on the ocean floor millions of years ago. Magma from the melted plate burst up through the crust as lava and hardened into rock. Each time there was an eruption, more and more lava piled up on the ocean floor. Finally the pile of lava reached up out of the ocean. This is how Mount Pelée was formed.

Warnings From Nature

In 1902, Saint Pierre was the busiest city in Martinique. There were many shops and markets in the town. People who lived there were used to living near Mount Pelée. The volcano didn't bother them at all. However, that year, in the beginning of May, very strange things started to happen around the volcano. A very fine dust called **ash** started to fall on the city like snow. The volcano let out puffs of smoke. People knew that these were signs that the volcano was erupting. They began to fear that the worst was still to come.

These people watched from a steamship as Pelée began to erupt in early May 1902.

Many people left their villages as Mount Pelée continued to erupt. Some of them fled to Saint Pierre, where they thought they would be safe.

Mud and Ash All Around

During the first week of May, ash from Mount Pelée fell all over the island of Martinique. In one town near the volcano, the ash fell so heavily that the roofs of the buildings began to collapse. The rumbling volcano also caused floods and mudslides that swept away animals, houses, and even people. Saint Pierre was a long way from the volcano. Many people came from other towns on Martinique to take shelter in Saint Pierre. Although the people of Saint Pierre were afraid, they thought they would be safe in their town.

13

Eruption

On the morning of May 8, 1902, Mount Pelée let out a type of eruption that had rarely been seen before anywhere else in the world. The volcano lit up with a flash like lightning and then split open in an explosion. A huge glowing cloud of gas, boiling mud, ash, and rock shot out of the volcano. Instead of floating into the sky, this cloud raced along the ground, straight toward Saint Pierre. The cloud was moving at about 310 miles (500 km) per hour. It burned or melted everything in its path. The heat from the cloud set factories in the town on fire. With fires from the factories blazing, the **temperature** in Saint Pierre quickly reached 1,652 degrees Fahrenheit (900 degrees C).

People looking through the ruins of Saint Pierre found metal clocks, silverware, and bottles that had been melted by the glowing cloud.

A glowing cloud, or pyroclastic flow, is able to travel over
mountains, forests, and even bodies of water.

A Glowing Cloud

Mount Pelée was unusual because it did not send out any lava flow when it erupted. Instead it released what scientists call a **pyroclastic flow**. The word "pyro" means fire, and "clastic" means broken. The pyroclastic flow was the cloud made of fire and broken rocks that swept over Saint Pierre. Another name for pyroclastic flow is "glowing cloud." People did not know about pyroclastic flow. They only worried about lava coming to their town. Saint Pierre was far enough from the volcano that it was not likely that lava would reach them. The pyroclastic flow, though, could travel to places that the lava could not reach. The glowing cloud moved through Saint Pierre for three minutes, from 8:02 until 8:05 A.M. When it was over, the entire town of Saint Pierre was gone and almost 30,000 people were dead.

17

Two Survivors

It's hard to imagine that anyone could live through such a terrible eruption. Most of the people killed by the volcano died instantly. The heat was too much for any human or animal to survive. Two people in Saint Pierre survived the eruption of Mount Pelée. A local shoemaker was badly burned but somehow lived through the heat and eruptions. The other person who lived through the eruption was a prisoner named Auguste Ciparis. He was left alone in the basement of the town prison. The thick stone cell kept him safe from the heat of the blast. Auguste lived for four days without food or water until he was rescued.

This is Saint Pierre after the eruption. People thought it was a miracle that anyone survived the terrible glowing cloud.

Martinique is still a popular place to visit. Saint Pierre, though, has never really recovered from the eruption of 1902.

What Happened Next?

Mount Pelée did not quiet down after May 8, 1902. The volcano entered into an **active period** after that terrible eruption. During the week after the glowing cloud swept through Saint Pierre, Pelée let out smaller explosions almost every day. During this time, thousands of people fled from towns near Saint Pierre and went to the other side of the island. In August, Mount Pelée let loose an eruption that was almost as big as the first one. This eruption killed 1,000 more people in Martinique. Saint Pierre was deserted for many years. People were afraid to come back. Today, almost 100 years after the eruption, only about 7,500 people live there. Mount Pelée is quiet now, but no one can forget the eruption of 1902.

21

We Never Stop Learning

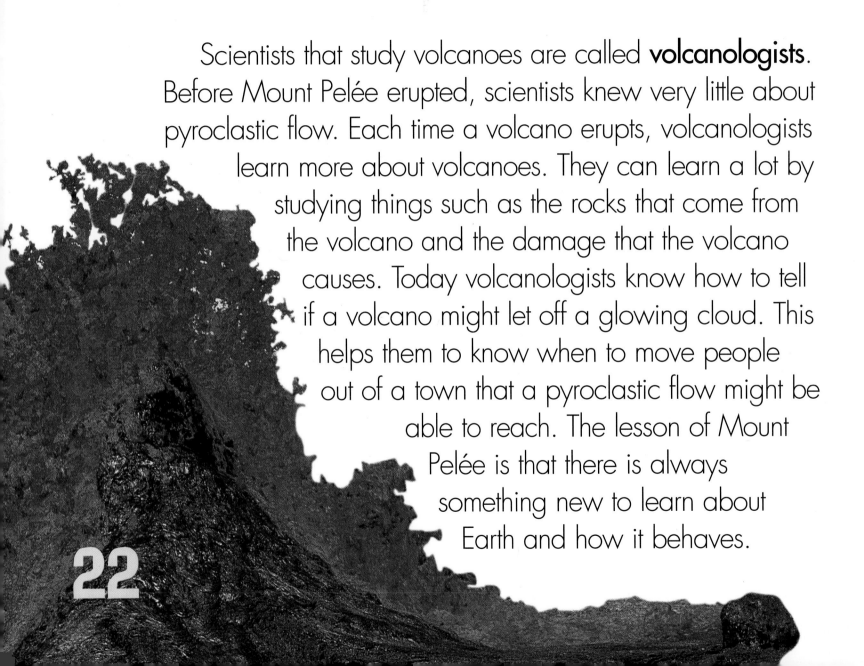

Scientists that study volcanoes are called **volcanologists**. Before Mount Pelée erupted, scientists knew very little about pyroclastic flow. Each time a volcano erupts, volcanologists learn more about volcanoes. They can learn a lot by studying things such as the rocks that come from the volcano and the damage that the volcano causes. Today volcanologists know how to tell if a volcano might let off a glowing cloud. This helps them to know when to move people out of a town that a pyroclastic flow might be able to reach. The lesson of Mount Pelée is that there is always something new to learn about Earth and how it behaves.

22

Glossary

active period (AK-tiv PIR-ee-od) The time when a volcano erupts.

ash (ASH) Tiny pieces of rock that shoot out of a volcano during an eruption.

core (KOR) The hot center layer of Earth that is made of liquid and solid iron and other elements.

crust (KRUST) Earth's top layer, where we live.

elements (EH-leh-ments) The basic matter that all things are made of.

eruption (ih-RUP-shun) The explosion of gases, smoke, or lava from a volcano.

lava (LAH-vuh) Magma that has reached Earth's crust.

magma (MAG-muh) Hot liquid rock found beneath Earth's surface.

mantle (MAN-tuhl) The middle layer of Earth.

plates (PLAYTZ) The moving pieces of Earth's crust.

pyroclastic flow (py-roh-KLAS-tik FLOH) An extremely hot cloud made up of gases, ash, and rocks, that comes from a volcano and moves along the ground.

temperature (TEM-pruh-cher) How hot or cold something is.

volcanologists (vol-kuh-NOL-uh-jists) People who study volcanoes.

Index

Web Sites

To learn more about volcanoes and Mount Pelée, visit these Web sites:
http://volcano.und.nodak.edu/vwdocs/volc_images /img_mt_pelee.html
http://vulcan.wr.usgs.gov/Volcanoes/WestIndies/Pelee/ framework.html

24